LONDON

TRAVEL GUIDE

The Ultimate Pocket Guide to the City of Magic: Unveil the Best of the UK Capital's Hidden Gems and Iconic Landmarks. Everything you Need to Know Before Plan a Trip to London

STUART HARTLEY

© Copyright 2023. All Rights Reserved.

The publication is sold with the idea that the publisher is not required to render accounting, officially permitted or otherwise qualified services. This document is geared towards providing exact and reliable information concerning the topic and issue covered. If advice is necessary, legal or professional, a practiced individual in the profession should be ordered.

- From a Declaration of Principles which was accepted and approved equally by a Committee of the American Bar Association and a Committee of Publishers and Associations.

In no way is it legal to reproduce, duplicate, or transmit any part of this document in either electronic means or printed format. Recording of this publication is strictly prohibited, and any storage of this document is not allowed unless with written permission from the publisher—all rights reserved.

The information provided herein is stated to be truthful and consistent. Any liability, in terms of inattention or otherwise, by any usage or abuse of any policies, processes, or directions contained within is the sole and utter responsibility of the recipient reader. Under no circumstances will any legal responsibility or blame be held against the publisher for any reparation, damages, or monetary loss due to the information herein, either directly or indirectly.

Respective authors own all copyrights not held by the publisher.

The information herein is offered for informational purposes solely and is universal as so. The presentation of the information is without a contract or any guarantee assurance.

The trademarks that are used are without any consent, and the publication of the trademark is without permission or backing by the trademark owner. All trademarks and brands within this book are for clarifying purposes only and are owned by the owners themselves, not affiliated with this document

TABLE OF CONTENTS

INTRODUCTION 5

CHAPTER 1: INTRODUCTION TO LONDON 7

    OVERVIEW OF LONDON'S HISTORY, GEOGRAPHY, AND CULTURE..10

    ESSENTIAL INFORMATION FOR FIRST-TIME VISITORS........15

CHAPTER 2: GETTING AROUND LONDON......................20

    TRANSPORTATION OPTIONS 25

    TIPS FOR NAVIGATING THE CITY'S TRANSPORTATION SYSTEM..29

CHAPTER 3: ACCOMMODATIONS IN LONDON 31

    OVERVIEW OF DIFFERENT TYPES OF ACCOMMODATIONS 35

    HOW TO AVOID TOURIST TRAPS AND GET THE BEST DEALS WHILE TRAVELING 43

CHAPTER 4: SIGHTSEEING IN LONDON.........................45

    TOP TOURIST ATTRACTIONS...53

    OFF-THE-BEATEN-PATH DESTINATIONS AND HIDDEN GEMS 57

CHAPTER 5: LONDON'S FOOD AND DRINK SCENE.....................59

    OVERVIEW OF THE CITY'S DIVERSE CULINARY SCENE.......61

    RECOMMENDATIONS FOR LOCAL RESTAURANTS AND BARS 63

CHAPTER 6: SHOPPING IN LONDON 70

    SCAM-PREVENTION STRATEGIES AND ADVICE FOR LOCATING TIIE BEST DEALS 75

CHAPTER 7: LONDON'S CULTURAL SCENE..................77

    RECOMMENDATIONS FOR MUST-SEE SHOWS AND EVENTS81

CHAPTER 8: LONDON DAY TRIPS 83

RECOMMENDATIONS FOR DAY TRIPS BASED ON DIFFERENT INTERESTS 87

CHAPTER 9: LONDON FOR FAMILIES 89

TIPS FOR TRAVELLING WITH CHILDREN IN LONDON 91

FAMILY-FRIENDLY ATTRACTIONS AND ACTIVITIES 93

CHAPTER 10: PRACTICAL INFORMATION FOR TRAVELERS ... 95

SAFETY TIPS 101

TIPS FOR BUDGETING AND SAVING MONEY DURING YOUR TRIP 103

CONCLUSION 106

INTRODUCTION

There are two major financial centers in the western world, one of which is London, and the second-place city is New York. There are several reasons why people visit London, and it is the western world for visitors, serving as the UK and England's capital.

London is one of the world's most vibrant and diverse cities, with a rich history that stretches back thousands of years. London is a hub of culture, commerce, and creativity, attracting millions of visitors annually.

London is a fascinating city with something for everyone. Its many neighborhoods, top-notch restaurants, and extensive cultural past make it a must-see for anybody with even a passing interest in history, art, literature, music, or the performing arts, not to mention the business community.

London is a large city with a reputation for absorbing newcomers and turning (some of) them against it. There are many incredible things to see and do in London, so long as you're willing to look past the trash and the (supposedly) sketchy subterranean system.

The British city of London is one that never gets old. London is an expensive place to live in or visit. However, don't give up since you can still visit London on a budget; you must ensure you receive value for your money rather than the absolute lowest price.

It need not be as pricey as you thought to see Big Ben or the Queen Mother in London. If you prepare carefully and with good judgment, seeing the vibrant guards of Buckingham Palace may be as inexpensive as it gets.

London is one location that harmoniously blends the nostalgic past and the current, enticing you to go there.

London would be one of the contenders for the "global capital" title if there were such a competition since it is both historic and modern, diversified, dynamic, and cutting-edge. If you're considering a city trip to London, this guide will give you some ideas to include on your itinerary.

This London travel guide will give travelers the best guidance to visit top tourist attractions.

There are numerous places of interest in the city. Every first-time visitor will be perplexed by the dizzying array of options.

You will get the proper information about attractions from this guide. This guide will help you locate the ideal locations and avoid visiting every location to determine whether it is appropriate for you to attend.

Let's get started!

CHAPTER 1: INTRODUCTION TO LONDON

To this day, London is the United Kingdom's and England's undisputed administrative heart. It is one of the world's most significant urban areas, celebrated for its long history, varied cultural offerings, and exciting nightlife. As one of Europe's largest urban areas, its population of nearly 8 million makes it a major metropolis.

Many international corporations and media outlets call London their home. This city has numerous museums, galleries, and theaters of international caliber.

London, one of the world's financial powerhouses, is among the most sought-after travel destinations. A singular allure and throbbing charisma completely enthrall the British capital.

Once, the major capital was considered the region's economic hub. The city demands an exceptional level of perplexity. The city, located along the River Thames, has attractions for visitors of all ages.

With more than 200 linguistic variations, it is an astounding fusion of civilizations. London is overflowing with tourist attractions, including double-decker buses, the lovely shores of the Thames, and endless greenery. The city isn't exactly known for its tranquil beaches, remote islands, or snowy cliffs, which are said to be the most enticing tourist locations. Yet, London nonetheless draws millions of visitors every year from all over the world.

London is a bustling metropolis that offers something for everyone. London has many attractions, including the Tower of London, the London Eye, Buckingham Palace, the British Museum, and the National Gallery.

The city has 33 boroughs, each with unique characters and attractions. The most famous areas of London include Central London, home to many of the city's major attractions and shopping districts, and the East End, which has a more diverse and creative vibe.

London is a center of innovation and creativity, with a thriving music, art, and fashion scene. This region contains some of the world's finest educational institutions, drawing brilliant minds from all over the globe to come here to further their education.

London is known for its excellent public transportation system, including the famous London Underground (or Tube), buses, and taxis. The city has several airports, including Heathrow, Gatwick, and Stansted, connecting it to worldwide destinations.

Many people visit London specifically to enjoy the city's stunning parks. Some popular parks include Hyde Park, St James's Park, and Regent's Park, great places to relax, exercise, or picnic.

London is not just a fantastic tourist destination, but also a fantastic place to go shopping. The best shopping areas include Covent Garden, Camden Market, and Oxford Street, and these areas offer various shops, from high-end boutiques to vintage and thrift stores.

London is a very safe city for tourists. The city has minimal crime, making it safe for tourists to wander around.

However, being aware of your surroundings and keeping your belongings safe is always good.

London is a fascinating city with something to offer everyone. Whether you're interested in history, culture, shopping, or nightlife, London is sure to have something that will interest you.

OVERVIEW OF LONDON'S HISTORY, GEOGRAPHY, AND CULTURE

London dates back to ancient times and over 2,000 years; the Romans founded it in 43 AD. It has been England's capital city since the 12th century. Over the centuries, London has played a major role in many important historical events, including World War II.

The city has been inhabited for over two millennia and has played a significant role in the development of Western civilization.

During the Middle Ages, London became an important center of trade and commerce, and the city continued to grow and flourish in the following centuries.

In the 19th and 20th centuries, London became a global economic and cultural hub, and today it remains one of the world's most important cities.

London is in southeastern England, bordered by the River Thames to the south. The city is divided into several boroughs with distinct characters and attractions. The central part of London is known as the City of London, which is the historical and financial heart of the city. Some of London's most recognizable landmarks are in Westminster, while Camden is well-known for its thriving arts and music communities.

London is known for its rich cultural heritage, with many museums, art galleries, theatres, and other cultural institutions. In addition to Buckingham Palace and the Tower of London, London is also home to other notable buildings that have made London famous worldwide.

London is equally well-known for its diverse population, with people from around the world calling the city home. This has led to a vibrant and eclectic cultural scene with a wide range of cuisines, festivals, and traditions in the city.

Culture in London also includes its illustrious music scene, which has spawned legends like The Beatles, The Rolling Stones, Pink Floyd, and Adele. The city is also home to numerous music festivals, including the British Summer Time festival in Hyde Park and the Notting Hill Carnival, which celebrates Caribbean culture.

Aside from its traditional cultural offerings, London is known for its cutting-edge contemporary art scene, with numerous galleries and exhibitions showcasing the latest in contemporary art and design.

The city's diverse food scene, with many restaurants offering worldwide cuisine. London has also seen the rise of the gastropub, a type of pub that offers high-quality food alongside traditional drinks.

London's culture reflects its rich history and diverse population. The city's diverse population has created an environment rich in history and tradition.

Today, London is a diverse and multicultural city with a large population worldwide. The city's music, art, and culinary cultures are diversified and thriving because of this diversity.

WEATHER

London's weather does not frequently experience highs and lows. On the other hand, London experiences heavy rain, on average, nine to ten days per month. No matter when you travel, be sure to bring some waterproof clothing; you'll probably be pleased you did.

April: Spring is a lovely time of year in London and around England. London is a green city; its parks and gardens burst with colorful, fragrant life in the spring. When temperatures are milder, planning a trip for early spring may be more beneficial, rather than waiting until the warmer summer months when fewer people would visit.

Summer: London enjoys a pleasant and beautiful summer typical of England. Seldom do temperatures rise over 75°F.

For this reason, hotel and airfare prices tend to be higher than usual during this period. On the other hand, this time of year is typically busier and more exciting than others.

Fall: The weather in the fall is mild and rainy, just like the summer. Put off your trip until the fall to escape the crowds and take advantage of the warmer temperatures.

Winter: Although it can get chilly, on average, winter temperatures rarely drop below 30°F. Christmas is celebrated widely in England, where cheery markets can be found. As the setting for Charles

Dickens's A Christmas Carol, London will surely put you in a merry mood come December.

ESSENTIAL INFORMATION FOR FIRST-TIME VISITORS

As a first-time visitor to London, you have got to know how to connect with your host. Americans connect very differently than the inhabitants of London, and the English, as a whole, do. Londoners prefer to maintain a respectful distance from one another and practice more reserved forms of courtesy.

In contrast, an American is likelier to talk with a stranger on the street and ask them how their day went within the first few minutes of meeting them. It's merely a variation in cultural conventions; don't take this to mean that people are being aloof or unpleasant when you meet them. Discuss topics other than work or family, such as movies, TV shows, books, travels, etc.

The following are some essential information for first-time visitors:

TIME ZONE

During the winter, it is Greenwich Mean Time; otherwise, it is British Summer Time (as of the beginning of Daylight Saving Time).

THE IDEAL TIME TO VISIT LONDON

London's weather is generally mild and rainy throughout the year, so the ideal time to visit will depend on your travel preferences. Those searching for Christmas markets and authentic holiday cheer will like the winter season for its beauty and celebration. At the same time, summer, spring, and fall are ideal for enjoying the parks and making the most of London's walkability.

VISA REQUIREMENTS:

Many nationalities citizens can visit the United Kingdom visa-free for up to six months.

However, checking the UK government's visa requirements is important to confirm whether a visa is required for your country of origin.

CURRENCY:

The currency used in London and the United Kingdom is the pound sterling (GBP). It is recommended to exchange currency before arrival or to use ATMs in London to withdraw cash, as exchanging money at airport bureaus or in tourist areas may incur higher fees.

LANGUAGE:

London speaks English as its main language, and visitors are unlikely to encounter significant language barriers.

However, London is a diverse city with a large immigrant population, and it's possible to encounter different accents and dialects.

SAFETY:

As with any large city, visitors should take precautions to ensure their safety, such as being aware of their surroundings and avoiding carrying large amounts of cash or valuables. Sticking to well-lit, busy areas at night and avoiding walking alone in unfamiliar areas is also recommended.

ELECTRICITY:

The electricity supply in London is 230 volts, and the plugs and sockets are of the Type G British standard. Visitors may need an adapter to use their electrical devices, which can be purchased at many electronics stores or online before arrival.

EMERGENCY SERVICES:

In an emergency, visitors can dial 999 or 112 for police, fire, or ambulance services.

THE BEST SOURCES FOR BOOKING IN LONDON

These are the businesses I like to use when I travel. They routinely outperform their rivals in pricing, customer service, and value. Overall, they are superior. They are the businesses I use the most and always start with when looking for travel discounts.

Skyscanner is my preferred search engine for flights. They look up obscure websites and low-cost carriers that larger search engines frequently overlook.

They are, without a doubt, the most suitable starting point.

Hostelworld is the top website for finding accommodations since it has the most options, the best search engine, and the largest selection.

The greatest overall booking site, Booking.com, consistently offers the lowest and most affordable prices. They offer the most options for affordable lodging. They have consistently had the lowest prices of all the booking websites in my tests.

HostelPass: With this brand-new card, you may save up to 20% on hostels all around Europe. It's a fantastic approach to cutting costs. Also, they keep introducing additional hostels. I've always desired something like this and am happy it is a reality.

A sizable internet marketplace for tours and excursions is called Get Your Guide. In cities worldwide, many tour alternatives are available.

If you plan to travel extensively by high-speed or long-distance trains while in Europe, get a rail pass. I've saved hundreds of dollars each time I've utilized a rail pass, which I've done three times. The math makes sense.

The Guy is the world's most comprehensive resource for train travel, and they have the most detailed knowledge about train schedules, fares, and conditions. Consult this site if you're planning a lengthy or extraordinary train trip.

Rome2Rio - This website lets you see the most efficient and affordable routes from Point A to Point B. It will provide every path you can take to travel there by bus, rail, airline, or boat, along with how much it will cost.

FlixBus - FlixBus offers services between 20 countries in Europe for as little as 5 EUR! Internet, outlets, and a free checked bag are all available on their buses.

SafetyWing: For long-term and digital nomad travelers, SafetyWing provides easy-to-use plans at reasonable prices. They are ideal for those traveling because they offer affordable monthly rates, excellent customer service, and a simple claims procedure.

LifeStraw is the brand I always turn to for reusable water bottles with built-in filters to guarantee the quality and safety of the water I consume.

Unbound Merino - They produce travel clothing that is compact, strong, and simple to clean.

Use this company for bike tours: Fat Tire Tours! They offer entertaining, engaging excursions conducted by knowledgeable local guides. You can tour all the major attractions without going bankrupt!

BlaBlaCar is a ridesharing website that enables you to share rides with verified local drivers in exchange for petrol contributions. You only ask for a seat, they grant it, and you proceed. Compared to using the bus or rail, it's more affordable and fun!

Take Walks - This walking tour provides exclusive access to sites and locations. They have some of England's greatest and most educational tours, and their guides are awesome.

Apps to Download

- London Tube Live:
- The Pub Finder
- London Theatre Direct
- London Pass

CHAPTER 2: GETTING AROUND LONDON

The UK's capital city is a sight to behold. Since this city is home to Europe's largest airport, Heathrow, getting it is not difficult. Due to this, it has the benefit of being served by most airlines worldwide. There are several options for getting to London Paddington, and the cost will depend on your choice.

Due to its lack of intermediate stations, the Express Rail can frequently transport you there in about 15 minutes. The London Tube is the most expensive and takes the longest, typically an hour. If you're carrying lots of stuff or have a family, it can be easier to take a taxi. You can hail a black cab, which is more expensive but always available, right off the street, or reserve a smaller cab, which usually operates by appointment only.

If you're from a European city like Paris, you may use the high-speed rail instead of flying. If you like, you might also use the long-distance bus. Even if it's not usually a good idea, driving into the city center is one way to get there. One of the world's most extensive transportation networks is present in the city.

Even still, walking is the greatest way to explore the city because London only seems large on paper. Walking would be a delight because the city is what you would term compact. Cycling is always a choice, even if it's not always the greatest.

London is a vast city with many different neighborhoods and attractions, so it's important to plan your transportation ahead of time to ensure you can make the most of your visit.

London has an extensive public transportation system, including buses, trains, and the famous Underground. With 11 separate lines covering most of London, the Tube is one of the most practical and inexpensive methods to get around the city.

The city is also pedestrian-friendly, with many areas accessible on foot, and taxis and ride-hailing services like Uber are also available.

Visitors can purchase an Oyster Card or a Travelcard to save money on transportation. You can take a taxi or utilize a service like Uber, and you can pay for rides with an Oyster card or contactless payment.

In London, you may easily hail a cab or reserve one ahead of time. Black cabs are the iconic London taxis and are easily recognizable, but visitors can also use ride-hailing services like Uber or Lyft for more convenience and flexibility.

The greatest method to see all London offers is on foot, as the city is incredibly accessible. Many of London's famous landmarks and attractions are close together, and visitors can easily walk between them.

London has a bike-sharing scheme called Santander Cycles, which allows visitors to rent bikes for short periods. The bikes are available at docking stations throughout the city, and the scheme is a great way to explore London's many parks and neighborhoods.

London is situated on the River Thames, and many ways exist to explore the river and its surroundings.

The River Bus service is operated by Transport for London and offers a scenic way to travel along the River Thames. The service operates from several piers along the river, and visitors can use an Oyster Card or contactless payment to pay for fares.

Viewing London from the ocean is a unique and unforgettable adventure. Several companies offer cruises along the River Thames, ranging from short sightseeing trips to dinner cruises with live music and entertainment.

Water taxis are a more expensive but convenient way to travel along the river. They offer a flexible service and can pick up and drop off passengers at various points along the river.

From its headwaters to its terminus at the Thames Barrier, the Thames Path is a hike of 184 miles. Bicycles can be rented, and the Thames Path, with its beautiful views of the river and the city, can be explored by visitors.

In addition to the River Thames, several parks and green spaces in London offer a break from the city's hustle and bustle. Some popular parks include Hyde Park, Regent's Park, and St. James's Park. These parks offer a variety of activities, such as walking, cycling, boating, and picnicking, and are a great way to experience London's natural beauty.

The public transit network in London is comprehensive and user-friendly, making it simple for tourists to get around the city and its environs.

TRANSPORTATION OPTIONS

London has a comprehensive public transportation system, including buses, trains, and the famous London Tube (the "Underground"). Visitors can purchase an Oyster Card or a Travelcard to save money on transportation, and taxis and ride-hailing services like Uber are also available.

Here is an overview of the different options:

THE TUBE:

The Tube, as the London subway is often called, is an easy and quick method to get around the city. Eleven lines make up the system, connecting virtually the entire city, and each line is color-coded. The Tube is open from early morning until late night, and trains run approximately every 2-5 minutes during peak hours. Visitors can purchase an Oyster Card or a contactless payment card to pay for their journeys on the Tube.

Tube riders have it easy because the system is extensive and well-maintained. The fee for the Tube varies depending on the time of day, the payment method used, and the number of zones you go through. In contrast, many American transportation systems charge per ride or travel duration. To make your journey on the Underground more convenient, consider buying an Oyster card, MetroCard, or SmarTrip Card.

Each of the nine boroughs is serviced by one of the eleven lines of the Underground system. There are maps of these locations available at every Tube stop. Zone 1 is home to most of London's must-see landmarks and the downtown core.

Monday through Saturday, the Tube is open from 5 am to midnight. On the weekends, customers can take advantage of late-night services. It would help if you still were prepared to hail a cab or use a rideshare app after midnight in London.

BUSES:

London's bus network is extensive, and buses run throughout the day and night. While slower than the Tube at rush hour, buses provide an excellent opportunity to explore the city from ground level. Visitors can use an Oyster or contactless payment card for bus fares.

TAXIS:

London's black cabs are world-famous and can be hailed on the street or picked up at designated taxi ranks. Taxis can be more expensive than the Tube or buses, but they offer a convenient and comfortable way to travel around the city.

NATIONAL RAIL:

The National Rail network serves destinations outside of London and is a good option for day trips and exploring the surrounding areas. Visitors can purchase tickets in advance or on the day of travel at train stations.

PRIVATE HIRE VEHICLES:

Private hire vehicles like Uber are also widely available in London. They can be booked using a smartphone app and offer a more affordable option than traditional taxis.

However, it's worth noting that private hire vehicles can't be hailed on the street like black cabs.

WALKING:

London is a pedestrian-friendly city, with many areas accessible on foot. There are several walking tours to get out and see the sights without renting a car.

CYCLING:

London has an extensive network of cycle lanes and bike-sharing schemes, such as Santander Cycles ("Boris bikes"). Visitors can rent a bike using a credit or debit card and explore the city on two wheels. Cycling can be a great way to see the city's sights, but following the road rules and wearing a helmet is important.

London's transportation network is reliable and easy to use, making it simple for visitors to get around the city.

TIPS FOR NAVIGATING THE CITY'S TRANSPORTATION SYSTEM

The London subway system is complicated yet manageable if you know what you're doing. For first-time visitors to London, navigating the public transit system can be a daunting experience.

Map out your travels: Using a map or transit app to plan your journey, you may save time and prevent getting lost.

Take advantage of Oyster Card discounts: You can use your Oyster Card to pay for rides on the London Underground (the Tube), buses, and other public transportation. It's more cost-effective than buying tickets at the station and can be loaded with more money whenever needed.

Take the Tube; it's the best method to get around London quickly and easily. Most of the city is serviced by 11 separate lines, with trains departing every few minutes. Traveling on the Tube during rush hour is not recommended because of the high volume of people using the system.

It would help if you tried to avoid traveling in London during rush hour because it might get very crowded. Weekdays are typically busy between 7:30 and 9:30 in the morning and 4:30 and 7 in the evening.

Use one of London's many buses; they go almost everywhere. Buses are a convenient and frequently less congested alternative to the

Underground (or "the Tube"). A bus ride can be paid for with your Oyster card.

Get on the Docklands Light Railway (DLR): The DLR, or Docklands Light Railway, is an automated train line that runs through the East End of London. It's a great way to go about the Docklands area, and you can see some amazing sights along the way.

Take a right where you stand: When riding the Tube's escalators, those who wish to stand should do so on the right side, making room on the left for those who wish to walk.

Watch your stride and be aware of the space between the platform and the train when entering or exiting a Tube.

Using a taxi or Uber outside of rush hour is best. With less traffic, a car service like Uber or a taxi can be cheaper and more convenient.

Take the Subway: Some of North and East London are serviced by the London Overground train network. Useful for getting to places that aren't directly accessible via the Tube system.

Discover the streets and parks of London on foot or two wheels. Plan your route with a map or navigation software to avoid getting lost.

Don't bother driving; navigating London's heavy traffic is a hassle if you can, take public transit instead of driving.

Using these suggestions as a guide, you should have no trouble getting around London and taking advantage of its many attractions.

CHAPTER 3: ACCOMMODATIONS IN LONDON

London has many accommodation options, from budget hostels to luxury hotels. Popular destinations include Central London, South Kensington, and Covent Garden.

London has many accommodations to suit all budgets, from luxury hotels to budget hostels. Finding affordable accommodations in desirable locations in London can be challenging, but it's not impossible.

These recommendations should help you find comfortable and affordable accommodation in London.

Choose your location wisely: London is a large city, so choosing a convenient location is important. Consider factors like proximity to public transportation, restaurants, and attractions.

Look for accommodations outside of central London: Central London can be expensive, so consider looking for accommodations in areas a bit further out. Zones 2 and 3 have plenty of affordable options, and you can still easily access central London using public transportation.

Book in advance: London is a popular tourist destination, so booking your accommodation well is a good idea to ensure availability and get the best prices.

Booking your accommodation in advance can often help you save money. Book early because many hotels and hostels offer discounts for early bookings.

Use price comparison websites: To compare the costs of different hotels easily, you can use a third-party website. This can help you find the best deals on accommodations.

Consider alternative accommodations: There are many alternative accommodations in London, such as hostels, guesthouses, and Airbnb rentals. These options are often more affordable than hotels and can provide a more unique and authentic experience.

Stay during off-peak seasons: Accommodation prices in London can be high during peak seasons, such as summer and around major holidays. Consider visiting during off-peak seasons to find more affordable accommodations.

Negotiate for a lower rate: Some accommodations may offer a lower rate if you stay for an extended period. It doesn't hurt to ask, so try negotiating for a better deal.

Join loyalty programs: Many hotel chains and booking websites offer loyalty programs that provide discounts and perks for frequent travelers. Consider joining these programs to save money on your accommodations.

Check online reviews: Before settling on a hotel or hostel, it is wise to read over comments left by former visitors. This can give you a good idea of what to expect and help you avoid unpleasant surprises.

Consider alternative accommodations: Besides traditional hotels and hostels, London has many accommodations like Airbnb rentals, serviced apartments, and guesthouses. These can be a more affordable and unique option for travelers.

Look for deals and promotions: Keep an eye out for deals and promotions on travel booking sites or through hotel loyalty programs. As a result, you could potentially spend less on lodgings.

Consider your budget: A firm and fair plan for where to stay in London is crucial. Consider staying in a budget hostel or looking for a hotel in a less central location to save money.

Finding affordable accommodations in desirable locations in London takes a bit of effort, but it's possible. Consider what else is out there, and plan and use a service that compares prices to get the greatest hotel deal possible. You can find the ideal, budget-friendly accommodation in London with just a little preparation.

Following these guidelines, you should have no trouble finding a room in London that suits your requirements and budget.

OVERVIEW OF DIFFERENT TYPES OF ACCOMMODATIONS

London offers a wide variety of accommodations, each with its advantages and disadvantages. In London, there are many hotels to choose from. Several dates back over a century, but if you're seeking the greatest hotel in London, you'll need to conduct a thorough search. You must pick a hotel in the right location that offers a good bargain and satisfies all your needs. Nearly every region of the city that is meant to be a tourist destination has hotels.

What follows is a brief overview of some of the most frequent types of lodging:

Hotels: London has a vast selection of hotels, ranging from budget to luxury. Hotels are a great option for travelers who want the convenience of on-site amenities like restaurants, room service, and concierge services.

Due to the wide variety of hotels available in London, you can save money on lodging. Many are significantly better than others, but they will cost more. Even if they are not five-star hotels, the average hotels in London are highly pricey.

Any standard hotel at a nearby tourist destination will save you more than $200 per night. The convenience of going everywhere you want to go is the only benefit of staying at these pricey hotels. The less expensive ones are farther from London, so you might have to take a double-decker bus or taxi. You can save more money by staying at these hotels farther away; most offer complimentary dinners and a continental breakfast.

It should come as no surprise that London has enough hotel rooms to accommodate the population of dozens of major cities worldwide, given that it is one of the most sought-after travel destinations in the world and is not to be missed!

The surprise would be that most of these hotel rooms are reserved far in advance, necessitating cautious planning to find a fantastic hotel at the ideal cost.

Although there are dozens of them, using a website to compare pricing and availability might be a smart method to achieve so.

Alternatives to Hotels

Globetrotters, St. Christopher's Inn, and YHA are the locations to visit if you're seeking hostels. All of them are centrally placed in London and only somewhat more expensive than very upscale places. Avoid using any agencies, and try to make your hotel reservations directly. You can use the internet to find the websites of the hotels, hostels, and inns that interest you.

You can benefit from a hostel if you're youthful and trendy. Although direct privacy is lacking, it is far less expensive than a typical motel. Always book in advance rather than a few days before your trip, and remember that the weather in London will likely cause you to remain in and spend a lot of time in your accommodation. This is not a vacation to a tropical location with resort hotels and swimming pools. The most important things are having a tidy bedroom, a nice bathroom, and a comfy bed. But please avoid locking yourself in your room for lunches or dinners. Try going outside to find a nicer restaurant that intrigues you. You'll discover that London boasts many great eating establishments, cafes, and bakeries.

Now that this is on your calendar, it is best to consider staying in a less expensive hotel in London rather than splurging on pricey and opulent lodging.

London is an extremely pricey place. Yet, most of London's tourist attractions are free to visit for anybody, resulting in significant savings. Nonetheless, spending money on travel and hotel is still necessary. Finding the ideal lodging in the United Kingdom can be challenging, but if you persevere, you will succeed. We can still reduce our everyday expenses and save money by paying attention to simple details.

TOP HOTELS

LA SAVOY

Because it is the only hotel of its caliber on the Thames, La Savoy has become famous worldwide for its luxurious accommodations. Even if you don't end up staying here, it's worth your time to stop by and take in the spectacular architecture and dramatic design of the first hotel in London, built specifically as a luxury hotel.

NED

Once a bank that went empty, The Ned opened its doors to guests in 2012 as a luxury hotel. Your stay at The Ned will be more of an adventure than a comfortable haven from your London explorations. It contains eleven different restaurants, all decorated in a 1920s manner. Massages and vitamin IV infusions are just two of the spa services available at The Ned. If you're a young couple or a group of friends looking to travel in elegance, the Ned is a great alternative. It's a bit more hip than your typical 5-star, but it still has character.

COTTAGE IN THE WOODS

The Chiltern Firehouse was a cozy little place when it wasn't used as a firehouse. Twenty-six room types, including standard rooms, lofts, and suites, are available, each with a working fireplace. A Michelin-starred restaurant offering seasonal menus is The Chiltern Firehouse. The Chiltern Firehouse provides a one-of-a-kind, cozy atmosphere that makes you feel just at home, even when you're far from it.

GORING

The Goring, a premium hotel in the same family for almost a century, features 69 rooms with unique decor. The Goring, located on the same street as Buckingham Palace, epitomizes a stay there. The Goring features a high-quality on-site restaurant and bar and a variety of flexible vacation packages to suit your individual needs.

11. CADOGAN GARDENS

Built as four separate townhouses in the late 19th century, 11 Cadogan Gardens is known for its unique and eccentric interior, which contains winding staircases and corridors. Because of its location in posh Chelsea, the hotel is convenient to several of London's most visited landmarks, including Hyde Park, Harrods, and the Saatchi Gallery.

ROSEWOOD

Convenient to both the British Museum and Covent Garden, the Rosewood is a five-star hotel with opulent, traditional furnishings. The five-star hotel, originally built in the Edwardian style, has undergone thorough renovations that successfully blend the old with the new. Enjoy a contemporary take on afternoon tea in the Mirror Room, decorated with works by British sculptor Antony Gormley, before heading out into the heart of London. It is recommended that guests of the Rosewood check room availability as far in advance as possible, especially during the hotel's busiest times of the year.

LANESBOROUGH INN

The Lanesborough started as a grand country mansion. Still, now it's a five-star hotel with a Michelin-starred restaurant, a private spa and fitness center, a cognac lounge, and award-winning afternoon tea service. The Lanesborough's gorgeous and homey furnishings make it a popular choice among travelers looking for a high-end hotel.

Budget travelers and backpackers often stay in hostels since they are less expensive than hotels. You can find hostels with dorm-style sleeping arrangements or private rooms with shared bathrooms, and most of them also have common areas like kitchens and living rooms for guests to use.

Renting a vacation home can provide you with the space and amenities of a hotel while feeling more like being at home on your trip.

Apartments and whole houses are available, and each has perks like Wi-Fi, a washer and dryer, and a kitchen.

Serviced apartments combine the best features of a hotel (such as cleaning and a front desk) with those of a vacation rental (such as more space and independence) to create an ideal accommodation option for business and leisure travelers.

Bed & Breakfasts are smaller, typically family-run hotels with a more intimate atmosphere. They are a terrific opportunity to experience the hospitality of a new place and often include breakfast.

Guesthouses: Guesthouses are small hotels or B&Bs offering a more intimate setting than larger ones. They often have fewer amenities but can offer a more personalized experience.

By understanding the accommodations available, travelers can choose the option that best fits their needs, budget, and travel style.

HOW TO AVOID TOURIST TRAPS AND GET THE BEST DEALS WHILE TRAVELING

It can be difficult to find good bargains and avoid falling into tourist traps in a city as vast and well-visited as London. To make the most of your trip, keep the following in mind:

Do your research: Before you go, research the attractions, restaurants, and accommodations you're interested in to discover any potential scams or tourist traps. Look at what other customers say and get suggestions from locals and tourists.

Book in advance: Booking tickets or tours can save money and help avoid long lines at popular attractions.

Look for local discounts: Many attractions and restaurants in London offer discounts for locals or visitors who purchase tickets in advance or online.

Avoid tourist areas: While staying and eating in popular tourist areas is tempting, these places often charge higher prices for lower-quality experiences. Venture out to more local areas to find authentic and affordable options.

Use public transportation: Traveling to London by taxi or tourist bus may get pricey. Use public transportation like the Tube or buses to save money and get a more authentic experience.

Check for free events: London has many free museums, parks, and events worth visiting. Check local listings or ask locals for recommendations.

Following these suggestions, you may save money and avoid tourist traps in London. Stay flexible and open to new experiences; you'll enjoy exploring this vibrant city.

CHAPTER 4: SIGHTSEEING IN LONDON

Everything a major city with so much history and culture should have, and more, is right here in London. As a result of climate change, London now has pleasant, even hot, summers that are perfect for sightseeing.

Even though the Queen and the London Eye are at the top of most people's lists, the city's historical and modern attractions are practically endless. When discussing London or England in general, rain inevitably arises.

Like many other extremely old towns, London was originally built on one bank and then both of a river, the River Thames, making a river cruise a terrific way to view most of the city's highlights.

From a riverboat, you can see many of London's famous landmarks, including Westminster Abbey, Big Ben, the Houses of Parliament, the South Bank Arts Complex, a recreation of Shakespeare's Globe Theatre, the Tower of London, and more.

London is well-known not just for its proximity to the river but also for its numerous parks, where residents and visitors may escape the never-ending din of the city. St. James' Park is a beautiful park just behind Downing Street, the Prime Minister's official residence.

Amazingly, you can walk to Buckingham Palace (the official house of the Queen of Great Britain) down the Mall and still be in St. James' Park, despite passing Duck and even Pelican Ponds.

You can tell if she is home by looking at the Royal Standard flying over the Palace. If you want to visit the Queen "at home," you'll have to travel 20 miles west of London to Windsor Palace, where she loves to spend her time since it is quieter and has less pollution.

From the blue plaque commemorating the Oxford Street apartment where Jimi Hendrix died to the beautifully restored St. Pancras station, which now houses the International Rail (Channel Tunnel) Rail Service, London is a tourist's paradise because there is always something interesting around the corner.

Many of the world's most recognizable buildings and sites can be found in London. A few of London's top attractions are listed here.

The Tower of London and Tower Bridge

When you think of London, Tower Bridge is probably the first thing that comes to mind, not London Bridge.

While the Tower of London is known as a prison for those who have committed crimes, its history is fascinating. Visitors interested in the Tudor era can take advantage of free tours all day long that follows in the footsteps of Queen Elizabeth I.

The historical fortification that has served as a prison, royal Palace, and treasure vault; is the Tower of London. It is a UNESCO World Heritage site and the location of the world-famous Crown Jewels. The castle hosts numerous exhibitions that tell the narrative of the castle and its inhabitants, including the world-famous Crown Jewels.

Tower Bridge has been a popular tourist destination in London for over a century. The drawbridges, often called bascules, on this bridge, weigh more than a thousand tons each. Every expeditor who comes to London to take in the city's splendor must walk across the magnificent bridge at some point.

"The London Eye": The London Eye (the Millennium Wheel) was purpose-built to provide spectacular metropolis views. Because of its purpose as an observation platform, the wheel was constructed uniquely. The view from the peak is so beautiful that it draws millions of visitors each year, even though the attraction costs a pretty penny.

The London Eye is a popular tourist attraction. Having 32 pods to house over 10,000 guests per day is just one of the fascinating features of this attraction. There is no better way to see the city than from this vantage point. Tickets for this trip can be bought in advance online.

Buckingham Palace: Buckingham Palace is a popular tourist destination open to the public. To this day, the Changing of the Guard ceremony at the Queen's official house remains one of the most watched events in the country.

The British Monarchy and royal court reside at Buckingham Palace, making it home to one of history's most rumored powerful families.

This attraction is only open to the public for two months each year, during the summer months of August and September. The "changing of the guard" ritual is only held on specific days throughout the other two months of the year when tourists are welcome to visit.

St. James' Park is one of London's most well-known green spaces, located close to Buckingham Palace and perfect for relaxing after sightseeing. Those looking for Newcastle-Upon-football Tyne's (soccer) stadium will be disappointed. In particular, its ducks have gained widespread notoriety, but a small colony of pelicans can also be seen there.

Westminster Abbey is a Gothic church where numerous monarchs have been crowned, and Prince William and Kate Middleton recently tied the knot.

Westminster Abbey's Gothic architecture and imposing presence are enough to wow history buffs. Since 1066, every English monarch has been crowned there, and many famous persons are buried there, such as Geoffrey Chaucer, the Unknown Warrior, Queen Elizabeth I, and Elizabeth of York. There are also some beautiful tributes to famous poets, artists, and writers at Westminster Abbey.

The seat of the British government and the location of the iconic clock tower known as Big Ben is located in a complex known as the Houses of Parliament. Most sightseeing trips include visiting the famous clock since it is a staple of any Instagram-worthy London feed and because it is conveniently located near other points of interest. Visitors must be UK residents to tour the tower.

Tate Modern is a museum devoted to contemporary art that may be found at a former power plant on the South Bank of the Thames.

The museum's roughly 80 million specimens are several dinosaur skeletons and other rare animal species.

More than 2,300 works of art from the 13th to the 19th centuries are on display at the National Gallery, which has gained international renown.

The National Gallery houses one of the world's greatest art collections, with pieces by such masters as Botticelli, Raphael, Titian, Rubens, Rembrandt, Cézanne, Monet, and Van Gogh. The 2,300 items in their collection are shown on a revolving basis, so you can see new and exciting things each time you go.

The British Museum is unique in that it houses both anthropology and art, unlike the National Gallery. The collections are organized by time period and place of origin, and rotating exhibitions explore different aspects of the human experience. Their collection includes about 8 million pieces, with many things only being removed for certain occasions, so be sure to check out the special displays.

The British Museum is home to one of the finest collections of Egyptian artifacts, marble friezes from the Parthenon in Greece, and the remarkable treasures the British amassed during their time as world rulers.

Exhibits at the British Museum come worldwide and span human innovation from prehistoric times to today.

The British Museum has more than eight million objects from all across the world.

All sorts of things are displayed in the museum, from ancient artifacts to global cultures to natural history. The Rosetta Stone, the Elgin Marbles, and the Sutton Hoo treasure are just a few of the museum's most renowned exhibits.

The iconic dome of St. Paul's Cathedral offers breathtaking views of the city below. When it was completed in 1690, St. Paul's Cathedral became one of London's most recognizable monuments, and it has kept the majority of its original stained glass to this day. Guests flock to the vast and exquisite mosaics, soaring Gothic architecture, and beautiful Cathedral library.

St. Dunstan was first built as a church in 1698, and it is located in what is now known as St. Dunstan in the East. Once a target of World War II firebombing, the area has since been transformed into a park with a peculiar and breathtaking beauty. The park may be small, but stepping foot inside it is like being transported to another planet. We strongly advise bringing a camera to capture the ivy-covered remains in all their photographic glory.

In London, you must see the famous Madame Tussauds Wax Museum. The Tussauds gallery is recognized worldwide due to its wax statues of numerous prominent people from all walks of life.

Sites of Wetland Significance in London: The London Wetlands Trust protects this scenic area at the city's heart. It's one of Europe's largest wetland areas, measuring over 43 hectares. Include this lively area of London in your travel plans.

The 350-acre Hyde Park in the heart of London is a sight to behold and deserves at least a day of your time. Events, historical buildings, walking tours, and lovely gardens make this a fun and interesting destination. For free speech and open debate, it is famous for Speakers Corner, which has been open to the public since 1872.

Shakespeare's Globe is a recreation of the original Elizabethan playhouse for which the Bard wrote and featured regular productions of his complete works. Shakespeare's time spent there further enhances the immersive experience that can only be found at the Globe.

Highgate Cemetery, part of Highgate Memorial Park, is home to over 170,000 interred souls and is sure to pique the interest of both history fans and ghost hunters. In addition to being a beautiful place to visit, it is also a natural reserve. Many well-known figures are buried here, and visitors can pay their respects at their graves. This includes Leslie

Hutchinson, Karl Marx, Douglas Adams, and George Eliot, to name just a few.

From museums and galleries to live performances and other forms of entertainment, London has something for everyone. There is a lot to see and do, so it's crucial to list your top priorities and stick to them.

TOP TOURIST ATTRACTIONS

London has a wealth of attractions, including world-famous landmarks like Buckingham Palace, the Tower of London, and the London Eye.

Many tourist attractions are located close to Buckingham Palace that you might like to visit. Trafalgar Square, the National Portrait Gallery, Covent Garden, and other attractions are all within a mile of each other.

Lunch in St James' Park is a pleasant respite in the middle of the day. Take your own if traveling on a tight budget because restaurants in London, like everything else, are pricey.

London has several excellent museums and galleries, including the British Museum, National Gallery, and Tate Modern. Many of these museums and galleries have free admission.

London is also home to many beautiful parks and outdoor spaces, including Hyde Park, Greenwich Park, and Richmond Park. These are great places to take a break from the city and enjoy the fresh air.

Since so many attractions and activities are available, it's natural to feel overstimulated. There are ways to navigate this challenge, and to assist you in facing this obstacle, consider the following advice:

Prioritize your must-see attractions: List the attractions you want to see before your trip. Prioritizing your must-see attractions can help you focus your time and energy on the most important things to you.

Consider a guided tour: A guided tour can be a great way to see multiple attractions in a short amount of time. A tour guide can also provide valuable insights into the history and culture of the city.

Plan your itinerary: Making the most of your stay in London is possible with careful planning. You might consider visiting related sites close together to save time and energy.

Stop and rest: Seeing all London's sights in one sitting is exhausting, so plan breaks in between. Don't overstretch yourself by trying to see everything in a single day. Instead, schedule pauses in your day and focus on the tasks.

Be open to unexpected experiences: Sometimes, the best experiences are not on your itinerary. Be open to exploring new neighborhoods, trying new foods, and stumbling upon unexpected sights.

Avoid peak times: Popular attractions such as weekends and holidays can be crowded during peak times. Consider visiting attractions during off-peak times to avoid crowds and have a more enjoyable experience.

These attractions can get crowded, so planning your visit and purchasing tickets is a good idea. The Tower of London is particularly popular during peak tourist season, so consider visiting early in the day or on a weekday to avoid the largest crowds.

The British Museum, on the other hand, is open late on Fridays, offering visitors a chance to explore the exhibits after regular hours.

Dealing with large crowds and long lines at popular destinations can be challenging, but there are ways to make the experience more manageable.

Here are some tips:

Arrive early: Arriving early can help avoid crowds and long lines. Many popular attractions in London open early in the morning, so consider getting there as soon as they open to avoid the crowds.

Book tickets in advance: Booking tickets can help you skip the lines and save time. Many popular attractions in London offer timed entry tickets that allow you to skip the general admission line.

Use a fast track or skip-the-line pass: Some attractions offer fast track or skip-the-line passes that allow you to bypass the general admission line. These passes can be more expensive, but they can save time and help you avoid crowds.

Be patient: Dealing with large crowds and long lines can be frustrating, but remaining patient and calm is important. Remember that you're not the only one dealing with the crowds, and try to focus on the experience rather than the waiting.

Explore alternative attractions: London is a city filled with countless attractions, and there are often many alternative attractions that are less crowded but just as interesting. Do some research and consider exploring lesser-known attractions to avoid crowds.

Dealing with large crowds and long lines at popular destinations in London can be challenging. In some cases, it is possible to lessen the severity of the situation. Arrive early, book tickets in advance, consider off-peak times, use a fast track or skip-the-line pass, be patient, and explore alternative attractions. With some planning and patience, you can have a rewarding and enjoyable experience in London.

OFF-THE-BEATEN-PATH DESTINATIONS AND HIDDEN GEMS

While London's top tourist attractions are worth visiting, the city has plenty of off-the-beaten-path destinations and hidden gems for visitors to discover. Here are a few examples:

Leake Street Tunnel: Located in the South Bank area, this tunnel is a mecca for street art lovers. Graffiti artists worldwide have painted the walls with colorful and thought-provoking murals.

Columbia Road Flower Market: This thriving East London market is open every Sunday and is a real treat for the senses. In this festive setting, guests can peruse a wide selection of flowers, plants, and gardening supplies.

Dennis Severs' House: Visit this one-of-a-kind museum in Spitalfields to learn about a fictitious family of Huguenot silk weavers from the 18th century. Visitors can wander through the house, filled with carefully curated artifacts and period furnishings.

Highgate Cemetery: Several notable people, including Karl Marx and George Eliot, are buried in this vast North London cemetery. The cemetery's history and architecture can be explored by taking a guided tour.

Little Venice: This picturesque neighborhood near Paddington is named for its scenic waterways and narrowboat moorings. Take a boat ride or stroll along the canals to get a feel for the place.

Visitors can better appreciate the city's unique history and culture by exploring beyond the typical tourist sites.

CHAPTER 5: LONDON'S FOOD AND DRINK SCENE

London's food and drink scene is a vibrant and diverse melting pot of international flavors and culinary traditions. From traditional British pub fare to trendy gastropubs, street food markets, and Michelin-starred restaurants, there's something for every taste and budget.

One of the best ways to experience London's food scene is by exploring the city's many food markets. Borough Market, located near London Bridge, is one of the city's most famous markets and has operated for over 1000 years. The market offers a wide variety of fresh produce, artisanal cheeses, baked goods, and street food worldwide.

Other popular food markets include Camden Market, which features a range of international street food stalls, and Maltby Street Market, known for its specialty coffee shops and craft beer vendors.

London has many Michelin-starred restaurants, including The Ledbury, Core by Clare Smyth, and The Clove Club. These restaurants offer creative and innovative tasting menus featuring seasonal ingredients and global influences.

London's pub culture is also a must-try experience for visitors. Traditional pubs like The Churchill Arms, The Lamb and Flag, and The Ten Bells serve classic pub fares like fish and chips, bangers and mash, and Sunday roasts, along with a range of local beers and ciders.

London has plenty of dessert shops and bakeries to satisfy any craving. From the classic pies and tarts at The Hummingbird Bakery to the modern ice cream creations at Chin Chin Labs, there's no shortage of sweet treats.

London's food and drink scene offers visitors diverse and exciting options to explore and enjoy.

OVERVIEW OF THE CITY'S DIVERSE CULINARY SCENE

London has a diverse food scene, from traditional British pub food to international cuisine. You can find great restaurants in areas like Soho, Shoreditch, and Camden. Try traditional British fare like fish and chips, pie and mash, and a pint of ale.

London's culinary scene is a melting pot of international flavors and influences, reflecting the city's multicultural population. From traditional British pub fare to international street food, Michelin-starred restaurants, and trendy cafes, there's something for everyone in London.

Popular among Londoners is Indian cuisine, which may be found at any number of restaurants and curry houses. Brick Lane in East London is particularly known for its numerous Indian and Bangladeshi restaurants.

London is also famous for its traditional pub food, which includes dishes like fish and chips, bangers and mash, and Sunday roasts. Pubs like The Churchill Arms, The Lamb and Flag, and The Ten Bells are great places to try these classic British dishes.

In recent years, London has become a hub for street food, with numerous food markets and festivals throughout the city. Borough Market, Camden Market, and Maltby Street Market are just a few of the popular food markets in London, offering a range of international cuisines from around the world.

London has many Michelin-starred restaurants, including The Ledbury, Core by Clare Smyth, and The Clove Club. These restaurants offer creative and innovative tasting menus featuring seasonal ingredients and global influences.

London has various cafes, bakeries, and dessert shops, from artisanal coffee to modern patisserie. The Hummingbird Bakery, Crosstown Doughnuts, and Chin Chin Labs are just a few of the popular dessert spots in London.

London's culinary scene is diverse, exciting, and constantly evolving, reflecting the city's dynamic and multicultural population.

RECOMMENDATIONS FOR LOCAL RESTAURANTS AND BARS

Knowing that British takeout sandwiches are superior to their American counterparts is funny and reassuring. Grab a sandwich from a fast food business if your day is too hectic for a sit-down lunch.

London has a diverse and active nightlife, with countless pubs, clubs, and other venues open into the wee hours. Shoreditch, Camden, and SoHo are all fantastic places to spend a night out on the town.

Some great London eateries and watering holes are listed below.

Franco Manca is a popular pizza chain in the area, known for its sourdough pizzas created with fresh, high-quality ingredients.

The Palomar: The Palomar is conveniently located near Trafalgar Square and several of London's finest museums. You can enjoy a meal of modern Jerusalem cuisine in a beautiful, mosaic-decorated setting. Order the octopus with harissa oil glazing or the Bayt al Maqdis Chicken if you want to try the artichoke chips independently.

This hip Soho eatery has an open kitchen and serves contemporary dishes from the Middle East and North Africa.

Hawksmoor is a franchise of steakhouses that is well-known for its premium, British-raised beef, and vast drink list.

With its flowery exterior and old-world allure, the Churchill Arms is a popular watering hole among Kensington residents.

The Blind Pig is a speakeasy in SoHo known for its unique and original cocktails and private atmosphere.

Nightjar is a 1920s-themed speakeasy in Old Street's underground market that features a wide selection of specialty cocktails and regular live music.

The Ned is a members-only club in the heart of London's financial district that features several public restaurants and bars, including a rooftop lounge with 360-degree views of the city.

Located near Fleet Street, Ye Olde Cheshire Cheese is a great example of a classic English pub that dates back to the 17th century.

The Bermondsey Beer Mile is a fantastic spot to try local brews and chat with fellow beer nerds.

Singburi is a hidden treasure of a Thai restaurant with a rotating menu of authentic and delicious curries, noodles, and seafood. Don't simply get your standard Pad Thai for takeout; try something new! (as delicious as Pad Thai is). That crispy omelet of theirs, the Kai Jeow, should go well with that (with oysters).

It's no secret that the staples of this popular restaurant with a sustainable attitude are fresh seafood, small plates, and bread. Large quantities of the best bread you'll ever eat. Please stop by for a croissant or sandwich, enjoy some of their small plates, or purchase a loaf of bread in advance to assure a delicious start to each morning of the workweek.

Noble Decay, with its seasonal wine bar and classic British menu, is a swanky eatery that puts the lie to the stereotype that British food is boring. Even if wine isn't your thing, you should check out this restaurant because they have an extensive wine selection and offer creative, innovative interpretations of classic British dishes.

Lyle's: Lyle's offers an ala carte lunch, so you and your pals can sample various dishes before settling on a few to share. There are limited options for each of the three courses on tonight's prix fixe dinner menu. The environment is lovely and private, making it ideal for enjoying your peaceful meal.

As a small, eco-friendly fish restaurant in Covent Garden, Parsons prides itself on its clear, ever-current menu. When it comes to updating classic British flavors for a contemporary audience, Parsons is unrivaled. They serve delicious sticky toffee pudding if you have room for dessert after your wonderful fish pie.

This Turkish cafe, Mangal Black Axe, may be small, but it makes up for its stature with its one-of-a-kind touches, such as its specialized buns (hot cross buns but with pentacles). Black Axe Mangal has a strong rock soundtrack, so even the excellent meal isn't taken too seriously. The lack of silence is offset by the fact that it is, above all else, pleasurable. Black Axe's edible glitter, clever dish names, and excellent beer selection make it a premier party spot.

If you're looking for Roti King and you're at Burger King, I'll warn you now that it's in the basement. And "hidden gem" isn't just a metaphor because you'll be treated to some of the finest Malaysian cuisines you've ever experienced. If you can't locate the queue of folks waiting for their chicken murtabak and char kuey teow, you should look for it.

Shoreditch Dishoom: No list of London restaurants would be complete without at least one recommendation for Indian food. While most are wonderful, one must have at least one recommendation for Indian food to be considered comprehensive.

Dishoom is a chain of Indian restaurants in London known for its tasty and inventive meals that take inspiration from the cuisine of Bombay's classic cafes.

Dishoom is one-of-a-kind and has attracted a loyal customer base thanks to its airy, Bombay-style decor, picturesque veranda, and original dishes. Remember that chicken tikka masala is a sweet dish in England, so if you're looking for a savory option, you might want to try gunpowder potatoes or marsala prawns instead.

HOW TO SEARCH FOR APPROPRIATE FOOD OPTIONS THAT MEET RESTRICTED DIETARY REQUIREMENTS

You may find vegetarian, vegan, gluten-free, and halal food in London. Here are some suggestions for locating meals that meet particular dietary requirements:

Find a good dining spot by doing some homework ahead of time. Find eateries that cater to your dietary needs by doing some research. Look up the restaurants' online menus or social media pages to see if they offer options for customers with special diets.

Inquire about suggestions: Inquire with the locals or the hotel staff for recommendations on restaurants that cater to special diets.

It's important to read food labels: If you have special dietary requirements, it is important to read them when grocery shopping.

Try looking for health food stores, vegan markets, or businesses that sell only gluten-free products; London is full of these and other specialist food stores.

Download some restaurant apps: Numerous apps can assist you in finding solutions that meet your dietary requirements. Some apps like Happy Cow and AllergyEats can help you locate restaurants that provide safe food for those with allergies.

Ensure your order is exactly what you want: Be precise about your dietary restrictions when placing a restaurant order. Make the waiter or waitress aware of any dietary restrictions or allergies you may have.

If you put in the time and effort, you may easily find restaurants in London that cater to your unique dietary demands.

Do your homework before you go out to eat, get recommendations from people you trust, read labels, seek out specialty food stores, use food apps, and be as detailed as possible when placing your order.

Thanks to these pointers, your dining experiences in London can be satisfying and appropriate.

CHAPTER 6: SHOPPING IN LONDON

London has various stores, from upscale malls to flea markets. Oxford Street, Regent Street, and Covent Garden are all fantastic places to do retail therapy.

London has a variety of shopping districts, each with unique character and offerings.

London is a great place to go shopping because it has so many unique stores, marketplaces, and brands. Here are some tips and recommendations for shopping in London:

Oxford Street: More than 300 retailers, including major department stores like Selfridges, John Lewis, and Debenhams and popular high street brands like Topshop, Zara, and H&M, line this European shopping boulevard, which attracts an average of 500,000 customers every day.

Regent Street: Regent Street is equally impressive; it connects to Oxford Street and features flagship stores for well-known brands such as Burberry, Kate Spade, Tory Burch, and many more. Regent Street was created to be the central shopping district of London. Although there may now be a few more, Regent Street was the first and perhaps best.

Bond Street is a high-end shopping district home to flagship locations of some of the world's most acclaimed fashion labels.

Covent Garden: Covent Garden, commonly known as the Covent Garden Market, is a beloved region home to a wide variety of restaurants and cafes, as well as oddball shops selling everything from vintage toys to vintage clothing. There are few finer places in London than Covent Garden to sip coffee and watch the world go by.

Covent Garden is a well-known market and district that has existed since its founding in 1694. Due to the lack of automobiles, a stroll through downtown is easy and pleasant. Covent Garden has several expensive restaurants and a vast selection of one-of-a-kind shops. Also nearby are the London Transport Museum and St. Paul's Cathedral.

Shops, boutiques, and market stalls abound in this pedestrian-friendly district, selling anything from gourmet chocolates to one-of-a-kind pieces of jewelry.

This exciting neighborhood is home to high-end boutiques and more reasonably priced market booths selling local arts and crafts, jewelry, and travel souvenirs.

Borough Market: The saying that "if it ain't broke, don't repair it" applies to London's marketplaces perfectly. Borough Market, one of the oldest institutions in the city, is huge and primarily focused on food. Although it wasn't incorporated as a city until the early 1900s, a section dates back to the 12th century. Prepare a sandwich and consider how pleased your ancestors would be with your wealth.

Notting Hill is a hip area with various restaurants, bars, and stores, including the world-famous Portobello Road Market.

Indeed, it's as cute as you'd hope. Notting Hill is a neighborhood in West London well-known for Portobello Road Market and the antique shops that line the street. The neighborhood also features chic restaurants, the beautiful Ladbroke Square Garden, and some of London's most picturesque neighborhoods.

Over 300 businesses, from high-end designers to popular high-street names, can be found at Westfield London, a massive shopping center in Shepherd's Bush.

Since it opened in 1791, Camden Market has been one of London's top tourist attractions. You can walk to nearby Regent's Park and the London Zoo from Camden Market, teeming with shops, bars, nightlife, and live music.

You can get to the London Zoo quickly on foot, but if you want to visit Queen Mary's Rose Gardens, you'll have to put in more time.

In this vibrant marketplace, you can find one-of-a-kind clothing, accessories, home decor, street food, and even live music.

Harrods, located in Knightsbridge, is a landmark store known worldwide for its high-end goods and services.

Brick Lane Market is a popular marketplace in East London to buy and sell antiques, unique foods, and artisanal goods.

Carnaby Street is a pedestrian street in the heart of Soho, known for its eclectic mix of high-end fashion boutiques and well-known international labels.

As the third and final commercial thoroughfare, Carnaby Street serves as a major retail hub in the area. Carnaby, located a few blocks north of Regent Street, is significantly less extensive and is primarily dedicated to the fashion industry, especially 1960s-era vintage clothing stores. Carnaby Street is much narrower than Oxford Street but still has many shops, restaurants, and cafes.

As a circular road junction that moves more leisurely than the rest of London, Seven Dials—sometimes included in the definition of Covent Garden—stands out as a truly unique area of London. Named for the seven sundials in the middle, Seven Dials is surrounded by about 90 shops and restaurants.

Canary Wharf is a commercial hub with a wide selection of stores, eateries, watering holes, and a sizable shopping mall stocked with luxury and high-street labels.

You may discover many high-end labels at bargain prices at Bicester Hamlet, a designer outlet village near London.

Due to its many unique stores, bookstores, and cafes, Marylebone High Street is a wonderful place to spend an afternoon shopping, reading, and people-watching.

There are many high-end stores in Knightsbridge, including the renowned Harrods department store, Harvey Nichols, and the boutiques along Sloane Street.

Several other locations of the famous, enormous bookstore Foyles are just as convenient, but the most beautiful one is in Soho, near Charing Cross. Due to its massive size, beautiful architecture, and extensive book variety, Foyles attracts many people who don't consider themselves readers.

SCAM-PREVENTION STRATEGIES AND ADVICE FOR LOCATING THE BEST DEALS

Following these guidelines can help you find the best sales and avoid being ripped off while shopping in London:

Research before you buy: Look up the average prices for the items you want to buy and compare them across different stores to find the best deals.

Shop during sales: London has several major sales events throughout the year, including the Boxing Day sale (December 26) and the January sales. Many stores also offer discounts during the summer and winter holidays.

Visit outlet stores: Several stores outside central London offer discounted designer goods, such as Bicester Village and Hackney Walk.

Use discount vouchers: Many stores offer discount vouchers that can be found online or in local newspapers and magazines.

Beware of scams: Be wary of sellers offering counterfeit or stolen goods and street vendors selling overpriced souvenirs. Stick to reputable stores and markets.

Bargain wisely: Haggling is uncommon in London but acceptable in certain markets and shops. If you do bargain, be polite and respectful.

Check the return policy: Check the store's return policy before purchasing, especially if buying from a small, independent store.

Use a credit card: Credit cards can offer extra protection for purchases, as you can dispute charges if there is a problem with the item or the seller.

CHAPTER 7: LONDON'S CULTURAL SCENE

London's cultural offerings are diverse and world-renowned, and the club scene in the city is well-known and celebrated. With so many options, it may satisfy any taste, from indie to rhythm n' bass.

It would help if you tried to attend several iconic clubs but enter the smaller, grungier clubs hidden beneath a railway arch to get a true sense of London.

Even more of London comes to life at night. In addition to enjoying some wonderful free live music in the cafés and bars, visitors may see the thrilling sight of the riverscape illuminated by laser lights and frequently by fireworks.

Ask some folks who appear interested in your interests for advice. Contrary to popular belief, Londoners are much nicer in reality.

London has a vibrant cultural scene, with many museums, art galleries, theatres, and music venues. Here are some highlights:

Museums: The British Museum, the National Gallery, Tate Modern, and the Victoria & Albert Museum are just a few of London's many excellent museums. These museums cover various topics, from art and history to science and technology. These institutions showcase a wide range of art and artifacts worldwide.

Many museums in London are free to enter, making them accessible to all.

Installation art is displayed in the enormous turbine hall of the Tate Modern, and depending on what is there, it may take your breath away. The galleries may feel crowded after entering that enormous area, yet there is much to see. Some items in the Tate will intrigue you even if you don't like art.

Art Galleries: Besides the major museums, London has many smaller art galleries showcasing contemporary and traditional art. Some popular galleries include the Saatchi Gallery, the Serpentine Gallery, and the Whitechapel Gallery.

Theatres: London's West End is famous for its theatres, which showcase a variety of plays, musicals, and other performances. Popular shows include The Lion King, Les Miserables, and Phantom of the Opera.

Music Venues: London has a thriving music scene, with venues ranging from small, intimate clubs to large concert halls. Some popular venues include the O2 Arena, Brixton Academy, the Royal Albert Hall, and the Roundhouse.

London is a great destination for music lovers, hosting concerts by international and local artists.

Festivals: London hosts various festivals and events throughout the year, including the Notting Hill Carnival, the London Marathon, the Chelsea Flower Show, the Winter Wonderland Festival in Hyde Park, and the Christmas markets.

Film festivals: London hosts several film festivals throughout the year, including the BFI London Film Festival and the London Short Film Festival.

Cultural Events: Besides the museums, galleries, theatres, and music venues, London hosts various cultural events, such as the annual London Fashion Week, the Frieze Art Fair, and the London Design Festival.

Historical landmarks: London has numerous landmarks, such as the Tower of London, Westminster Abbey, and St. Paul's Cathedral.

Parks and gardens: Hyde Park, Kensington Gardens, and the Royal Botanic Gardens, Kew, are just a few of London's many renowned green spaces.

Food and drink scene: London's food and drink scene is diverse and world-renowned, with a range of Michelin-starred restaurants, street food markets, and traditional pubs.

Street art: Popular street painters like Banksy and Shepard Fairey have contributed to London's vibrant street art scene. The East End is particularly known for its street art.

Literary events: London has a long history of great writers and literature and hosts many events yearly. The London Book Fair, the Bloomsbury Festival, and the London Literature Festival are just a few examples.

Comedy clubs: London has many comedy clubs showcasing up-and-coming and established comedians. The Comedy Store, the Soho Theatre, and the Leicester Square Theatre are popular venues.

London's cultural scene is diverse and vibrant, with something for everyone. Whether interested in theatre, art, music, or something else, you will surely find plenty to see and do in the city.

Anyone with even a passing interest in art, history, music, food, or any other cultural pursuit should make the trip to London.

RECOMMENDATIONS FOR MUST-SEE SHOWS AND EVENTS

London has a rich cultural scene, and there are always plenty of shows and events to choose from. Here are some recommendations for must-see shows and events in the city:

West End shows: The West End in London is home to some of the best theaters in the world. The Lion King, Les Miserables, and Phantom of the Opera are just a few examples of critically acclaimed productions.

Shakespeare's Globe: The Globe Theatre is a replica of the original theatre where William Shakespeare's plays were performed. The theatre hosts productions of Shakespeare's plays throughout the year.

Royal Opera House: This is the year-round stage for a wide range of performances from the Royal Ballet and the Royal Opera.

Notting Hill Carnival: The Notting Hill Carnival is Europe's largest street festival, celebrating Caribbean culture and music. The carnival takes place over the August bank holiday weekend.

Chelsea Flower Show: This Chelsea Flower Show is a world-renowned horticultural event showcasing the best garden design and landscaping. The show takes place in May each year.

Christmas markets: London's Christmas markets are a festive treat, with stalls selling gifts, food, and drink. Popular markets include Winter Wonderland in Hyde Park and the Southbank Centre Winter Market.

New Year's Eve fireworks: Launched from the London Eye and other famous sites, London's New Year's Eve fireworks display is one of the largest in the world.

There are countless other performances and events in London. Research online or at the local visitor's bureau for up-to-date listings and recommendations.

CHAPTER 8: LONDON DAY TRIPS

The day spent visiting the Tower of London will surely be one of the most memorable in London. Discover the lengthy and illustrious history of the British Monarchy, including some shady episodes. Visit the Crown Jewels and examine the carvings that the imprisoned members of the Royal Family left on the walls of their cells.

During your time in London, if you find yourself with some spare time, you can take several fantastic day trips to locations in the surrounding area. The following are some well-liked choices:

Oxford: Oxford, which can be reached by rail in a little more than an hour, is home to one of the most prominent universities in the world as well as numerous historic structures and museums.

Cambridge is a town in England home to several educational institutions and is famous for its gorgeous river, historic colleges, and stunning architecture. In addition, traveling to London by train takes little more than an hour to complete.

Stonehenge is an ancient monument that may be seen in Wiltshire, and it can be reached from London by train or automobile in about two hours. It is unknown what the monument's function is or how it was constructed, and all left is a ring of standing stones. Exhibits and guided tours inform visitors about the history of Stonehenge and the monument's significance, and visitors are welcome to explore the site.

The picturesque city of Bath can be reached by train from London in about an hour and a half. Bath is located in Somerset. The city is well-known for its Georgian architecture, Roman baths, and gorgeous countryside. Visitors get to see the city's many historic buildings and museums and the ancient Roman baths, which date back to the first century AD. In addition, the city is home to the Jane Austen Centre, which honors the life and writings of the well-known novelist by whose it is named.

The Pier, the Beach, and the Bustling Arts Scene Make Brighton the Famous Seaside Town It Is. It is around an hour's journey by rail from London.

Windsor Castle is a historic castle that can be seen just outside of London, and it holds the record for being the oldest and largest inhabited castle in the world. Visitors get to see the castle, its grounds, and the picturesque town of Windsor.

Canterbury is a city that dates back to the middle ages, and it is most well-known for being the location of Canterbury Cathedral, one of the most well-known Christian sites in the world. It is around a train ride of an hour and a half distant from London.

The Cotswolds is an area in England recognized for its gorgeous landscape, including rolling hills, lovely villages, and magnificent farmland. The trip to London takes approximately two hours by train or car.

Shoreditch is a trendy neighborhood in London home to various vintage shops, cafes, art galleries, and nightclubs. Neighborhoods featuring chain restaurants, fine dining businesses, and specialty coffee shops are popular places for younger people to settle down. Discover some of London's most excellent shopping in this neighborhood.

Kings Cross is the name of a neighborhood and a train station. Despite this, the old Kings Cross Station is a popular destination because it is conveniently located close to a Harry Potter-themed shop and a photo opportunity at Platform 9 34. The once heavily industrial neighborhood of Kings Cross has been completely revamped with the addition of gardens and other small green spaces.

Soho is a neighborhood that is known for its many lively theaters. In the West End, Soho is the place for any nightlife. Attend a show, go out dancing, watch a movie late at night, eat dinner, or do all the above. Because of its proximity to Trafalgar Square and the National Gallery, it is one of the most popular tourist destinations in all of London.

The West End is comparable to New York City's Broadway district. But don't let that fool you; it's not just productions from Broadway that are produced elsewhere. The West End is home to a thriving theater culture, regularly presenting world premieres of brand-new plays.

These are just a few day trips you can take from London. With so many options, you can choose a destination that suits your interests and schedule and experience England's rich history and culture beyond London.

RECOMMENDATIONS FOR DAY TRIPS BASED ON DIFFERENT INTERESTS

Here are some recommendations for day trips from London based on different interests:

History: If you are interested in history, you can visit the cities of Bath and York. Bath has a rich Roman history and is famous for its Georgian architecture, while York is home to one of the best-preserved medieval city walls in the world.

Nature: If you love nature, consider visiting the Cotswolds, the Lake District, or the South Downs National Park. The Cotswolds is a picturesque region with rolling hills and charming villages, while the Lake District is known for its stunning lakes and mountains. The South Downs National Park is perfect for hiking, cycling, or enjoying the beautiful scenery.

Culture: For a cultural experience, head to the university cities of Oxford and Cambridge or visit Stratford-upon-Avon, the birthplace of William Shakespeare. These cities offer a wealth of museums, galleries, and historic landmarks.

Theme parks: If you are traveling with kids or are a thrill-seeker, consider visiting the LEGOLAND Windsor Resort or the Thorpe Park Resort, both located just outside London.

Coastal towns: For a day trip to the seaside, head to Brighton, a vibrant and cosmopolitan town famous for its pier and beaches, or to the historic town of Canterbury, which boasts a magnificent cathedral and charming cobbled streets.

CHAPTER 9: LONDON FOR FAMILIES

London is a great family destination, with plenty of activities to entertain parents and children. Here are some recommendations for things to do in London with kids:

Museums: Many of London's world-class museums are free to the public. The British Museum, the Natural History Museum, and the Science Museum are all great options for families.

Parks: London has many parks and green spaces, which are perfect for picnics, games, and outdoor activities. Hyde Park, Regent's Park, and St James's Park are all popular choices.

Theme parks: As mentioned earlier, the LEGOLAND Windsor Resort and the Thorpe Park Resort are located just outside London and are perfect for families who enjoy theme park rides and attractions.

Zoos and aquariums: The London Zoo and the SEA LIFE London Aquarium are popular attractions for young families.

Harry Potter: For fans of the Harry Potter series, visiting the Warner Bros. Studio Tour London - The Making of Harry Potter is a must-see. The tour takes you behind the scenes of the Harry Potter movies and includes sets, costumes, and props.

River Thames: Take a boat tour along the River Thames to see London differently. The London Eye, a massive Ferris wheel on the

South Bank of the River Thames, offers spectacular views of the city below.

The West End: The West End is home to some of the world's best theatre productions. Many shows are family-friendly, including The Lion King, Matilda, and Wicked.

Food: London has a diverse culinary scene, and many restaurants cater to families. Jamie Oliver's Italian, Pizza Express, and Wagamama are all popular choices for families with children.

TIPS FOR TRAVELLING WITH CHILDREN IN LONDON

Traveling with children in London can be a fun and rewarding experience. Here are some tips to make your trip with your family as enjoyable as possible:

Plan: Research family-friendly activities and attractions in advance, and consider purchasing tickets or making reservations before your trip to avoid long lines or sold-out events.

Take advantage of public transportation: London's transportation system is family-friendly, and children under 11 can travel for free on the Tube, buses, and trams when accompanied by an adult.

Visit parks and playgrounds: London has numerous parks and playgrounds perfect for letting your children run around and burns off some energy.

Consider family-friendly accommodations: Look for hotels or vacation rentals that offer family amenities, such as cribs, high chairs, or family suites.

Engage your children in the culture: London has a rich cultural heritage and many ways to excite them. Consider taking them to museums or historical sites or attending a family-friendly theatre or music performance.

Try local food: London has a diverse culinary scene, and trying local food can be a fun and educational experience for your children.

Be prepared for the weather: London weather can be unpredictable, so pack appropriate clothing and gear for your children, such as rain jackets and umbrellas.

Take breaks: Schedule breaks throughout the day to allow your children to rest and recharge. This is a good opportunity to try local treats or snacks.

Following these tips ensures that your family trip to London is a memorable and enjoyable experience for everyone.

FAMILY-FRIENDLY ATTRACTIONS AND ACTIVITIES

There are many family-friendly attractions and activities to enjoy in London. Here are some recommendations:

The London Eye: A giant Ferris wheel offering stunning city views.

The British Museum is considered to be among the best museums in the world due to its extensive collection of priceless artifacts, including the Rosetta Stone and Egyptian mummies.

The Natural History Museum: A fascinating museum featuring exhibitions on dinosaurs, animals, and human evolution.

The Science Museum: An interactive museum where kids can learn about science and technology through hands-on exhibits.

The Tower of London: A medieval fortress with a long and storied history, including tales of kings and queens, prisoners, and even ghosts.

The Harry Potter Studio Tour: A must-visit for Harry Potter fans, this tour takes you behind the scenes of the films and lets you see the sets, costumes, and props up close.

The London Zoo: One of the world's oldest and most famous zoos, featuring a wide variety of animals, including lions, tigers, and gorillas.

The V&A Museum of Childhood: A museum dedicated to children, with exhibits on toys, games, and childhood throughout history.

The Diana Memorial Playground: A large, imaginative playground inspired by the story of Peter Pan, located in Kensington Gardens.

The Changing of the Guard: A ceremonial tradition that occurs daily at Buckingham Palace, where a new group of soldiers replaces the Queen's Guard.

London offers a wide range of family-friendly attractions and activities, ensuring that there's something for everyone to enjoy.

CHAPTER 10: PRACTICAL INFORMATION FOR TRAVELERS

London has so many exciting activities that picking the best ones can be challenging. This advice will help you make the most of your trip.

Prioritize your interests: List your interests and prioritize the activities or attractions that align with them. For example, prioritize visiting museums and galleries if you love art.

Read reviews: Read online reviews from other travelers to get an idea of what experiences they enjoyed and what they recommend. Websites like TripAdvisor and Yelp can be great resources for this.

Consider the time of year: Some experiences are better enjoyed at specific times. For example, visiting a Christmas market during the holiday season or watching the Wimbledon tennis tournament in the summer.

Mix popular attractions with off-the-beaten-path experiences: While visiting the popular attractions in London is essential, consider exploring some of the city's lesser-known areas. This will allow you to experience the local culture and avoid crowds.

Look for unique experiences: Consider unique experiences such as a food tour, a bike ride, or a street art tour. These experiences can provide a different perspective on the city and make your trip more memorable.

Consider your budget: Some experiences can be expensive, so consider your budget when choosing activities. Look for free or low-cost experiences like visiting parks or attending a street festival.

Ask locals for recommendations: Locals can provide valuable insights into the best experiences in the city. Strike up a conversation with locals or ask for recommendations at your accommodation.

Ultimately, the best experiences in London are the ones that align with your interests and make your trip memorable. Considering these tips, you can make informed choices and create a personalized itinerary that suits your preferences and budget.

STRUGGLING WITH LANGUAGE BARRIERS AND CULTURAL DIFFERENCES.

London is a diverse and multicultural city, and it's common to encounter language barriers and cultural differences when visiting.

Here are suggestions to help you face these obstacles head-on:

Learn some basic phrases: Learning some basic phrases in the local language can go a long way in helping you communicate with locals. Learning even a few words is a good first step since this will demonstrate your want to engage with the other person and help break the ice.

Use translation apps: Many can help you communicate with locals who speak a different language. Some popular options include Google Translate and iTranslate.

Respect cultural differences: Respecting them when visiting a new place is important. This includes things like dress codes, social customs, and religious practices. Research before your trip to learn about the local customs and traditions.

Ask for help: If you're struggling with language barriers or cultural differences, don't hesitate to ask for help. Locals are often happy to assist visitors and can provide valuable insights into the local culture.

Be patient and flexible: Dealing with language barriers and cultural differences can be frustrating, but remaining patient and flexible is important. Remember that you're in a new place, and things may differ from what you're used to.

Attend cultural events: London has a vibrant cultural scene. Attending events such as festivals and exhibitions can be a great way to learn about the local culture and meet new people.

It takes time and energy to adjust to London's language and cultural differences, but that's all a part of the adventure of visiting a new location. Learn some simple phrases, act politely, and don't be afraid to ask for assistance. If you go to London with an open mind and a willingness to learn, you'll have a great time.

ADJUSTING TO LONDON'S UNPREDICTABLE WEATHER.

Adjusting to London's unpredictable weather can be challenging, but there are ways to prepare for the ever-changing conditions. Here are some tips:

Check the weather forecast: Before you head out for the day, check the weather forecast. You'll be better prepared for the day if you know what to expect.

Dress in layers: The weather in London can be unpredictable, so it's important to dress in layers. This will allow you to adjust your clothing as the temperature and weather change throughout the day.

Bring a waterproof jacket and umbrella: Rain is common in London, so it's a good idea to bring a waterproof jacket and an umbrella, which will help keep you dry when it rains.

Wear comfortable shoes: London is a city best explored on foot, so wearing comfortable shoes is important. Choose shoes that are suitable for walking and can handle wet conditions.

Seek indoor activities during bad weather: If the weather is particularly bad, consider seeking indoor activities such as visiting museums, art galleries, or indoor markets.

Stay hydrated: Even if the weather is cooler, staying hydrated throughout the day is important. To stay hydrated, fill up a water bottle before you go and drink frequently.

It might be difficult to adjust to London's fickle climate, but there are steps you can take to mitigate its effects. Keep an eye on the forecast, dress in layers, pack a raincoat and umbrella, don't go outside if the temperature drops below freezing, and wear shoes that can withstand the terrain. This advice will help you have a more pleasant time in London, no matter the weather.

SAFETY TIPS

Like any major city, London has its share of crime, but it is generally safe for tourists. Keep your wits about you and your belongings safe, especially in crowded situations.

Feeling unsafe in unfamiliar areas or at night can be a common concern for travelers in any city, including London.

If you want to feel more secure, consider these suggestions.

Stay in well-lit and populated areas: Stick to well-lit areas with plenty of people, especially at night. Avoid poorly lit areas, deserted streets, or alleys that seem unsafe.

Plan your route: Stick to well-known and well-lit areas before leaving your accommodation. Avoid shortcuts through unknown or isolated areas.

Use public transport: Use public transport or licensed taxis instead of walking alone at night. Use trusted and licensed taxi services like Uber or black cabs.

Stay aware of your surroundings: Stay aware of your surroundings and be mindful of suspicious behavior. Keep an eye out for any emergency help points or police stations.

Don't carry large amounts of cash: Avoid carrying large amounts of cash or valuable items. Instead, use a card or mobile payment where possible.

Travel with a companion: If possible, travel with a companion or a group of people. There is safety in numbers; having someone with you is always better.

Use hotel safes: Keep your valuables, passport, and important documents in a hotel safe when you are not using them.

Remember to trust your instincts and be cautious. If you feel uncomfortable or threatened in any situation, remove yourself from it immediately and seek help. Taking these precautions makes you feel safer and more confident while exploring London.

TIPS FOR BUDGETING AND SAVING MONEY DURING YOUR TRIP

London is reputed to be one of the most expensive cities in the world, and if you are not careful, you can find yourself spending far more than you had intended.

The first item on that list is lodging; therefore, if you want to get the greatest offers and pricing, you must book enough rooms. In any event, there are several five-star hotels in London from which to select, and you only have to choose the option that best suits your financial situation.

Dining comes second, and just like in any other city, you can have a delicious dinner at a reasonable price. Nevertheless, if you prefer upscale dining, plan to spend at least 80 Euros on a good lunch and wine. That cost will likely quadruple if you select one of London's top eateries.

Most museums and other attractions are free; however, donations are frequently appreciated. Yet, other attractions, like the Madam Tussauds Wax Museums, are too expensive even though they are among London's top attractions.

Managing expenses and sticking to a budget is an important part of any trip to London.

Some suggestions for keeping your spending in check and your money in your wallet:

Plan: Before going to London, budget for your trip. Include all your expected expenses, such as transportation, accommodation, food, entertainment, and souvenirs. It's important to be realistic with your budget and allow unexpected expenses.

Look for discounts and deals: Many attractions in London offer discounts for students, seniors, or people with disabilities. Also, check for deals on websites like Groupon or LivingSocial for discounted tickets or vouchers for restaurants and activities.

Use public transportation: Public transportation in London is a cost-effective way to get around the city. Purchase an Oyster card, which allows you to use buses, trains, and the Underground at a discounted rate.

Prepare your meals: To save money, prepare some meals instead of eating out. You can save money by cooking your meals at many hotels and hostels. The opportunity to explore the local food market or supermarket is another perk.

Avoid tourist traps: Tourist areas in London can be expensive, so try to explore some of the less popular areas of the city. This will also allow you to experience the local culture and cuisine.

Limit souvenirs: Souvenirs can be expensive, so limit your purchases. Instead, consider taking photos or collecting small items like postcards or magnets.

Keep track of your expenses: Maintaining a spending log while traveling is smart. Use a spreadsheet or budgeting software to monitor your expenditure and make appropriate adjustments.

Overall, managing expenses and sticking to a budget in London requires some planning and discipline. Following these tips, you can enjoy your trip to London without breaking the bank.

CONCLUSION

London is home to some of the world's finest restaurants, an unequaled music scene, first-rate hotels, and a history that spans an extremely long time. Due to the high quality of England's public transportation, it is not difficult to get around London, a wonderful city to visit. Even if you spent a week or more exploring London, you still couldn't see everything, and that's just in one neighborhood.

The National Portrait Gallery, Trafalgar Square, the Tower of London, Tower Bridge, Kensington Gardens, and an abundance of cuisine, drink, shopping, history, and culture make the "Big Smoke" a natural magnet for tourists. Other attractions include the Tower of London and Kensington Gardens.

Traveling between the several intriguing neighborhoods comprising London is made simple and stress-free because of England's first-rate public transportation system.

I hope you have a wonderful time in London!

Made in United States
Orlando, FL
17 April 2023